Finding Your Destiny

A Guide for Your Ministry

Joe and Stephanie DeMott

A letter from Joe and Stephanie DeMott

Dear Reader,

This guide is intended for couples that want to teach the 8 Keys to Breakthrough: Victory in Your Marriage course (referred to hereafter as 8 Keys). We want this guide to be an inspirational resource, provoking your thoughts and leading you into prayer to seek what God is telling you.

Proverbs 3:5-6 (NIV)
⁵ Trust in the Lord with all your heart and lean not on your own understanding; ⁶ In all your ways acknowledge Him, and He shall direct your paths.

Matthew 6:33 (NKJV)
But seek first the kingdom of God and His righteousness, and all these things shall be added to you.

In 2014, after 29 years of ministering to marriages with another international marriage ministry, God called us out on our own. He was very specific in some things, but not specific in others. We knew for sure that we were supposed to get out in the world and preach the Word of God; and that we were still called to marriages and family. We knew it was going to be different, but we didn't know how different. Our purpose and vision is to reach every marriage whether they are going strong or in need of healing. We are also called to train Godly married couples to work together whether they are in ministry or not.

As you read through this guide, look at it as a foundation for some good ideas, but more importantly as a tool to help you reflect on what ministry is to you. What does it mean to you as an individual and as a couple? One thing we know for sure is every person is different and every couple is different. We all operate in different ways whether it's raising our children or helping our grandchildren grow. Everyone's "One Flesh" has its own attributes. When we bring culture into it there are even more differences that are unique to you as a couple. Most importantly we must always direct people to the word of God.

"YAHWEH NOT MY WAY"

Our only balance is the Word of God, not man's opinion or the world's opinion. His Word is our plumb line. So, think of this training aid as a tool to ignite the call on your lives. We want to make it possible for any Christian, Bible believing church to use our material and benefit from our experience. Our desire is to network with many churches and ministries.

Proverbs 16:11 (NIV)
Honest scales and balances belong to the Lord; all the weights in the bag are of his making.

Only God brings balance.

We know that many couples need structure, both in their own marriage and their ministry. There are also those that don't like structure. They have a desire to do things differently and flow in a way that makes the structured very nervous. We encourage both. Again, God made you unique:

Pray, Dream, and Do!

Our world vision for marriages is huge. It includes all biblical marriages between a man and a woman, marriages of all status and background, and we want YOU to be a part of it. But how do we reach all these marriages? We do it through the love of God. The greatest gift is love and we express it through our commitment to the Father and each other. We need to receive God's love in our own relationship in order to release it to others. So of course, your relationship with God is the most important, first individually and then your relationship and love for God together.

1 Corinthians 13:1-13 (NKJV)
¹ Though I speak with the tongues of men and of angels, but have not love, I have become sounding brass or a clanging cymbal. ² And though I have the gift of prophecy, and understand all mysteries and all knowledge, and though I have all faith, so that I could remove mountains, but have not love, I am nothing. ³ And though I bestow all my goods to feed the poor, and though I give my body to be burned, but have not love, it profits me nothing.

⁴ Love suffers long and is kind; love does not envy; love does not parade itself, is not puffed up; ⁵ does not behave rudely, does not seek its own, is not provoked, thinks no evil; ⁶ does not rejoice in iniquity, but rejoices in the truth; ⁷ bears all things, believes all things, hopes all things, endures all things.

⁸ Love never fails. But whether there are prophecies, they will fail; whether there are tongues, they will cease; whether there is knowledge, it will vanish away. ⁹ For we know in part and we prophesy in part. ¹⁰ But when that which is perfect has come, then that which is in part will be done away.

¹¹ When I was a child, I spoke as a child, I understood as a child, I thought as a child; but when I became a man, I put away childish things. ¹² For now we see in a mirror, dimly, but then face to face. Now I know in part, but then I shall know just as I also am known.

¹³ And now abide faith, hope, love, these three; but the greatest of these is love.

John 3:16 (NKJV)
For God so loved the world that He gave His only begotten Son, that whoever believes in Him should not perish but have everlasting life.

About Missionaries2Marriages

Core Values

1. **We must always point people to the Lordship of Jesus**
   We must deepen people's relationship with Jesus, not make them dependent upon us. We see people and situations through the eyes of faith. The Word of God is our guide.

2. **Strong Families that move in the Holy Spirit make strong churches**
   After believers are born-again, there is a second, distinct experience in which the Holy Spirit empowers believers (Acts 1:8). The power of the Holy Spirit changes the believer from within (Fruit of the Spirit) and flows out through the believer (Gifts of the Spirit).

3. **Marriage is a covenant**
   It reflects the covenant relationship between Jesus and the Church. Man and Wife agree to be faithful no matter what the other one does. It is unconditional. It is until death.

4. **Marriage between a man and a woman is God's plan for family**
   God intends for family to produce healthy sons and daughters in the image of their Heavenly Father.

5. **We are to bring the life of God's Word to all Nations**
   We are to bring the healing power of Christ to marriages and families of every Nation modeling transparency and the word of God.

6. **Marriage does not take away identity it enhances it**
   God brings out the best in us so when a marriage is challenged, we can rise to the occasion to see healing and wholeness.

7. **God sees families generationally**
   We should leave a legacy of Covenant and peace and a knowledge of God to the next generation.

8. **We are a body**
   We are to network with like-minded ministries and build the Kingdom of God.

Mission Statement

We commit to go to all Nations to preach the good news of the Gospel of Jesus Christ. We commit to teach Covenant Marriage everywhere we go in any realm that the Lord provides proclaiming healing for marriages and families. We commit to bringing the love of Christ to their families and marriages. God is always for reconciliation. Our mission is to bridge the gap between ministries with like vision, building up and bringing unity to the body of Christ.

Missionaries2Marriages Global Call

We are called to reach every couple in every nation.

Missionaries2Marriages has a global call to marriages. We believe strategies may be different across nations. We know that some nations may have to totally depend on others to finance their ministry while others may be able to sustain themselves. Our job is to leave no one behind. We commit to have excellent translations in as many languages as needed. We also commit to new creative ways to help fund the mission and help not only the families we minister to but the ministers that do the work.

Missionaries2Marriages is committed to reach every Nation with the love of Jesus and His healing power. We will reach the world with our marriage course, *8 Keys to Breakthrough: Victory in your marriage*. We will also use social media as well as any other means we can. We have coordinator couples all over the world expanding the vision. These couples will be connected to the ministry through relationship with Missionaries2Marriages by constant two- way communication and prayer. We will build relationship with like-minded churches and ministries to get the job done.

If you have a call to a certain nation, we will do our best to help you to fulfill that call. There are no boundaries as far as who can go where. The mission is to reach all people in all realms of influence.

We believe that video conferences are a great way to reach couples. You may already have a sphere of influence you can minister to in this way and stir up the gifts in couples and get them saved healed and delivered. Let's strategize! Be creative! Your mission field may be in your own neighborhood or you may have to get your passport. That's why you are Missionaries2Marriages

Covenant

Missionaries2Marriages believes and teaches Covenant. This is not negotiable. The marriage Covenant is a blood Covenant "'til death do we part", meaning that divorce is never the answer for a couple under any circumstances. If a couple divorces, each person is to remain single or be reconciled to one another.

1 Corinthians 7:11 (NKJV)
But even if she does depart, let her remain unmarried or be reconciled to her husband. And a husband is not to divorce his wife.

The Lord directed that this teaching be put in lesson three on forgiveness of *8 Keys* because this is where the issue can be resolved. Repentance and receiving the Lord's forgiveness is the key to healing of a divorce and of a remarriage while a former spouse is still living. Repent of the divorce and repent of the remarriage and let the Covenant you are in stand strong, so it does not happen again. You must also forgive yourself and whoever sinned against you that may have caused or played a part in a divorce.

We need to be aware that Christians in the Church today have many views on this subject and cannot stand in judgement but through God's grace bring truth. It is important to understand what the scripture really says about this issue. Many couples think they understand Covenant, only to have a divorce in their own family and suddenly, their own beliefs are challenged when they are faced with divorce directly. Missionaries2Marriages will not prevent you from teaching the course if you have doubts about this teaching, but we do ask you to teach it as it is written. Explain that it is what Missionaries2Marriages believes, even if you express your own concerns.

Whether you agree or disagree with this teaching, do not try and convince others that it is right. Please encourage them to take it home and pray together and learn to hear from God. If a couple you are ministering to is in a remarriage situation, let the Holy Spirit bring healing and restoration to them. It is the Holy Spirit's function to bring conviction, not ours. Even if you are ministering to couples not in a remarriage situation, the goal of Missionaries2Marriages is that all couples understand Covenant.

Our desire is to hold on to our beliefs and convictions and at the same time love those who do not have the same view. The goal of Missionaries2Marriages is to see marriages strengthened and restored. We are praying for God's standard for family to be lifted. We are not here to debate but to encourage couples to walk in unity. I (Stephanie) personally know the pain of being from a broken family. Our prayer is to stop divorce, through the power of Christ. We know through the study and applying of God's word family can received healing and wholeness.

Please study the Divorce and Remarriage section in Lesson 3 of "*8 Keys*" so you have a good understanding of the teaching. Please do not hesitate in contacting us personally if you have any questions.

Working Together

When working with your spouse in ministry and all areas of life, remember first and foremost the battle belongs to the Lord.

Matthew 11:29-30 (NKJV)

²⁹Take My yoke upon you and learn from Me, for I am gentle and lowly in heart, and you will find rest for your souls. ³⁰For My yoke is easy and My burden is light.

Your priority in working together as a couple is prayer. Pray first for your own marriage. You can't help anyone if your own marriage is a casualty of war. Focus on doing these things:

- Encourage one another
- Protect one another
- Listen to one another
- Pray for each other
- Honor one another
- Listen to God together
- Take time for one another

Study Scriptures
1 Thessalonians 5:11
Ecclesiastes 4:1
James 1:19,
Ephesians 18:19,
Luke 11:28,
1 John 5:14,
1 Peter 2:17,
Romans 12:10
James 5:16

Do not expose one another's weaknesses. There will be times when in teaching, ministering, or testifying that you will mention your own weaknesses, but that is much different than "telling" on each other.

Missionaries2Marriages understands that the man-and-wife relationship looks different in many cultures, but needs to line up with the word of God. We are not trying to change your culture, but we must insist that the husband and wife teach and minister together. That is the model we are displaying for the world to see. Of course, this can look different for every couple because every couple does ministry different in their own way. Don't let the devil get you to compare yourself to anyone else. Spouses should encourage each other in their unique giftings. We desire that you do these two things in your ministry:

1. Communicate with each other
2. Be One Flesh in leadership, not only in name but in actions

Your marriage is your most important ministry; please always remember this!

There are many ways you can present this course together. It can be done in a home group, weekend seminar or Sunday school. You can even use it one-on-one with a couple! How are you designed to minister? If your call is to disciple and train leaders, you can do that. You can minister to a group of couples and train them in the same sessions. Keep reading for more about logistics, strategies, and suggestions for how you can use this course.

Lead, Don't Control

The point is, Missionaries2Marriages wants you to use this course in the way God is calling you specifically to do ministry. Seek the Lord for how he is calling you to minister. Take time to pray and seek His guidance.

Styles of leadership will look different from church to church and nation to nation. Rather than implementing a specific structure or hierarchy of leadership to administer the course, Missionaries2Marriages wants couples and churches to implement it in the way that works most effectively for their community or region. You may have a way that you do things in your church or ministry and we release the course to you to use in your own way.

Together we sit in heavenly places

Our key word is "release". **RELEASE TO INCREASE.**

We want to release this course to you. Use it in the way God is calling you and increase the healing and restoring work of God in marriages and families. You are not "our volunteers".

Serve from the heart of God. We encourage you to influence others who respect you because you do your best to walk with the Lord and be an example. We will all fall short, but people know when you are genuine. You are valuable to the kingdom.

Think and pray about these questions:

1. What kind of person influences you?
   _____
   _____
   _____

2. How can you encourage others in their call?
   _____
   _____
   _____

3. How can you stay connected to those that you minister to?
   _____
   _____
   _____

4. What ways can you mentor couples that you have ministered to in an informal way?
   _____
   _____
   _____

Spiritual Abuse

Missionaries2Marriages does not claim to be an expert authority on this subject. We just have a few things for you to consider as you work with us or any other church or ministry. One characteristic of an abusive religious system is that the real needs of the people are lost. What is left is a never-ending quest by the leaders for personal fulfillment and happiness. There is a culture of paranoia, a fear of "Absalom", and suspicion of the very people doing the work of the ministry. Leaders may be identifying themselves with certain spiritual offices such as "Prophet" or "Apostle", but there is no evidence of fruit or integrity of character. Here are a few things to beware of and be prayerful if you notice these in ministry:

- You are consistently told, by your oversight (in any ministry), who you are and what you are like. This person always seems to know what is good or bad in your personality or character and doesn't have a problem with letting you know it.
- You are consistently told what is wrong with your children and that the way you interact with your children is incorrect.
- You consistently get the feeling that everything you do is wrong.
- You are consistently told that you are overprotecting your spouse.
- You are told to put ministry before your family.
- The target or focus of what you have been told to do constantly changes.
- You are asked to invest your money in a personal project or even a ministry project with a ministry leader. Make sure you are in agreement with your spouse and God. Seek counsel from a knowledgeable person. We do not mean offerings for ministry projects. We are talking about investments where there is a personal return promised or implied.
- A financial burden befalls you because of your dedication to ministry and you are told you are "doing it all for God".

Jeremiah 6:13-14 (NKJV)
[13] Because from the least of them even to the greatest of them, everyone is given to covetousness; and from the prophet even to the priest, everyone deals falsely.
[14] They have also healed the hurt of My people slightly, Saying, 'Peace, peace! When there is no peace.

Study Scriptures
Proverbs 16:11
3 John 1:2
Proverbs 11:1
Philippians 4:5-6

This is not a comprehensive study about spiritual abuse, but it is food for thought and much prayer. Look at the fruit of the ministry. If there are hurt people everywhere and no joy that is a clue that something may be wrong! When we walk free of spiritual abuse, we are free to excel in God's work. If we get caught and entangled in abuse, it weighs us down.

Our desire must be that everything we do is led of the Lord and not man. This will ensure we don't get "burned out" or deceived.

The Fivefold Ministry Gifts

The Bible gives us clear guidelines on the five-fold ministry. The concept and purpose come from Ephesians.

Ephesians 4:11-13

[11] And He Himself gave some to be apostles, some prophets, some evangelists, and some pastors and teachers, [12] for the equipping of the saints for the work of ministry, for the [a]edifying of the body of Christ, [13] till we all come to the unity of the faith and of the knowledge of the Son of God, to a perfect man, to the measure of the stature of the fullness of Christ;

Missionaries2Marriages believes it is important to understand the fivefold ministry, both the function and fruit associated with each of these five roles in ministry. The five giftings are summarized in the table below. The information in this table was taken from *The Making of a Leader* by Frank Damazio. This will help you identify your own gifting and that of others by knowing character traits and behaviors that relate to each gifting.

Gifting	Definition	Function	Reference
Apostle	Sent One, a delegate or ambassador, bearer of a commission	Establish local churches and ordain elders, bring forth revelation of the Word and to train and disciple ministries, to bring adjustment to counselors, to be a spiritual father to others	Ephesians 4:11 Corinthians 12:28 Acts 2:43
Prophet	Foreteller or God's Word and future events. Foreteller of God's word under inspiration from the Spirit. Mouthpiece or spokesman for God. An interpreter of God's word	Function in the office of a prophet, pronounce judgment, confirm direction of a ministry, to travel with apostles in team ministry confirming local churches	Ephesians 4:11 Ephesians 2:20 Acts 11:27-30 Acts 13:1-4
Evangelist	Preacher of the Gospel. Preacher having a harvesting ministry.	Train soul winners to win the lost through preaching and miracles, to work with apostolic teams in starting and establishing churches	Ephesians 4:11 Acts 21:8 2 Timothy 4:5
Pastor	Herdsman of God's people. An overseer of the Church. One who tends, guards, feeds, and guides the flock of God.	Feed and counsel the flock, to lead and oversee the flock, to identify with the flock	Ephesians 4:11 John 10:16 John 21:16 1 Peter 5:2,3
Teacher	Instructor of God's Word, one who imparts systematic knowledge, a teacher of other teachers	Established truth and doctrine from God's word, teach others how to teach, correct doctrine, balances the prophet's inspirational ministry	1 Corinthians 12:28 1 Timothy 3:2 2 Timothy 2:2,24

Encouragement:

We encourage you to seek out one of the many teaching on "Love Languages" and "Spiritual Gifting's" tests that are available online.

Teaching of the course

There are many ways to implement training and ministry. Whether you are ministering to couples or are called to pastor a church, Missionaries2Marriages desires to help you in what YOU as a couple are called to do. As you will see, we do not make strong distinction between training and ministry. We feel that as you minister to couples, they will be trained as well and realize whether they should minister to others or not. Building relationship with others is much more important. If the Lord does call a couple to teach others and/or teach *8 Keys*, then disciple them to be all God called them to be and help them do it.

The anointing on your lives is of the utmost importance and your specific giftings matter to the Lord. It matters to the couples you are ministering to and to Missionaries2Marriages. If you see yourselves as teachers of the Word of God and His principles, then teach. If you're giftings lean more towards facilitating, that's great. You can have the couple or group of couples read the lesson on their own and then go through it all together for explanation or ministry. The blue response sections in the manual can also be done by couples during the teaching or as homework. The "Treasured Time Together" homework at the end of the lessons is important for the couples to complete together on their own.

Missionaries2Marriages staff is a support system to you for any situation. It is our desire not to control the way things are done but still hold onto the vision that God gave for this ministry. There may be differences in how this course is used in different nations. Not everything has to be or should be the same. We are flexible with cultural and financial differences because we want to bring this course to as many people and nations as possible. We pray that your ministry can be self-sufficient, but we will help financially if it's necessary and funds are available.

The next section offers some suggestions for ways to present the course. There is no minimum or maximum requirement for the size of the group or seminar if that is how you are teaching this course. However, the content of the course cannot be changed. The standard of Covenant as well as walking and ministering as One Flesh are non-negotiable.

Strategies for Your Ministry

Home Group

A proven vehicle of ministry is the home group. This is a great way to get couples together and minister the course to them. You can do this in any structure that works for you and your couples. *8 Keys* has nine lessons including the introduction lesson. You can split those up any way you want. Take as long as you need to minister to those you are working with. Try not to wear yourself out by going late into the night. There are no restrictions on the number of couples in the group. Feel free to have fellowship in your meetings. One thing you can do is to use the 1st Lesson "Journey Ahead" as an ice breaker. Get to know the couples, maybe have a meal together.

Seminars or Conferences

You can teach the course to a large group on a weekend, over several hours, or spread out over one or two days.

Couple to Couple
You can teach the course to one couple at a time. Sometimes this is the only way a couple will be ready to receive so we should be open.

Ministering Online
You can do a small or large group online. Skype or ZOOM are good free tools to use for this. Facebook video messenger would also work. There are many conferencing programs available. Reaching couples is the goal! Some feel that this approach is not personal enough. We understand that concern, but in many cases, it is the only way to get the course to couples and you can make relationship with the couples online if you take the time to do so.

Training Centers
The course can also be taught in what is called a Training Center. A center can be set up in many ways. It can be part of a local church. A schedule can be set up on a consistent day and time and couples can take the class they need. You can develop a team of teachers to spread out the teaching responsibilities.

Self-Taught Couple
Couples are encouraged to go through the course together if they just want to purchase a manual for their own use. This is done best when they are accountable to another couple that can minister to them. We have had awesome testimonies of couples going through the manual on their own. We do not want to limit God with our rules.

Video Course

The entire "8 Keys" course is also available on video with Joe and Stephanie teaching every lesson. The course follows the manual and can be used along with the manual or without the manual. The course allows for pausing the video so couples can do the weekly exercises as they watch the course. So as with all that we have mentioned you can do this anyway that fits your time frame and logistics, at church or at home. You can do it weekly or in one or two sessions, whatever works for you and the couples in your group, session or conference. The course will be available on our website for a donation of $118.

Discounts will be available for churches and for manuals. Please inquire from our International Office at info@Missionaries2Marriages.com.

Notes

Finances and Partnering

It is the goal of Missionaries2Marriages to make the course available to everyone no matter their financial status. In the United States we ask for an offering of $18 a manual. Separate offerings taken during the course are not required, but of course accepted. If your church is using the course, they are welcome to take an offering for the church.

This ministry is funded by people like you. Missionaries2Marriages is seeking partners who will commit to giving $18 monthly or in multiples of 18 and invites you to partner with us financially and in prayer. In Hebrew, the related word Chaya means "life" or "long life", and is derived from the Hebrew word chai, meaning "life". It is a Jewish tradition to give gifts and donations in multiples of 18, which is called "giving chai". This is used in all giving, weddings, births, etc. So, as you consider giving to Missionaries2Marriages on a monthly basis, consider giving a multiple of $18 to bless marriages all over the world with "Life". We ask the Lord to bless you, your families, and marriages in return! We appreciate that you encourage people or organizations to partner financially and in prayer with us as well to expand the vision.

We have been able to reach many nations because of our willingness to help the Nations financially to succeed. We believe that there are nations and individual couples that are very thankful that others are willing to give so they can have healed and strong marriages.

The Lord has also allowed us to plant sewing centers in Pakistan and our desire is if there is a need to hep families in this way that we will continue to do this. The ministry has also helped individual leaders of M2M with medical assistance if possible.

Much of Missionaris2Marriages budget goes to ministering to couples in third world nations. In these nations Missionaires2Marriages must supply manuals and food for the couples to be at the training. We are praying for these nations to become self sufficient but our help is needed.

Missionaries2Marriages is a 501c3 ministry and gifts are tax deductible. You can find us on www.Guidestar.org for financial accountability. We promise to always have a Platinum Seal which is the highest seal.

Our Resources

8 Keys to Breakthrough: Victory in Your Marriage

8 Keys is our marriage course designed to be use in homes, churches, small groups, large groups, training centers, or just for individual couples. It has been translated into the following languages: English, Spanish, Portuguese, Italian, Urdu, Amharic, Russian, French, Chichewa, Arabic, German, and others. A premarital addendum is coming soon!

Our lessons include:

- Introduction: The Journey Ahead
- Key One: Walking in Unity
- Key Two: Covenant
- Key Three: Living in Forgiveness
- Key Four: Growing Together
- Key Five: Victorious Living
- Key Six: United in Love
- Key Seven: Breaking Free
- Key Eight: Value of Multiplication

Fan the Flame of Your Heart

This syllabus can be taught over a short time and used as a handout for a one-night event or an all-day marriage seminar.

The sections include:

- Condition of your Heart
- Covenant Love
- Discovering Oneness

Redemption: A Story of a Healed Marriage

In this booklet, Joe and Stephanie DeMott tell the story of their own testimony and how God healed their marriage. See below for endorsements from other pastors and missionaries.

Endorsements of "Redemption"

I have known Joe and Stephanie for more than twenty years and have ministered in marriage conferences several times with them. Their testimony of marriage restoration against all odds is extremely powerful and refreshing. In the current divorce culture, it is very encouraging to read a story of God's redemption for a marriage that no one thought could be healed. If you are struggling in your marriage, this book will greatly encourage you and embolden your faith in the living God to supernaturally heal your marriage just as He did for Joe and Stephanie. However, I encourage you not to only think of yourself, but to always have on hand several copies of the DeMott's book, Redemption, to give to other couples in need.

Craig Hill Founder - Family Foundations International
www.familyfoundations.com

Joe and Stephanie have condensed in this booklet the miraculous healing of their lives, marriage and family. This miraculous bending, blending and restoring of their lives, marriage and family has given hope to many as a result of their travels worldwide. Their transparency of the process of their own healing, through God's grace by faith in His word has given birth to hope in the hearts and lives of many over the years who have seen similar miracles in their lives, marriages homes and families. Their prayer and ours is that the Lord may be pleased to use their testimony to spark the same hope, faith and healing in the hearts of many that, "with God nothing shall be impossible"!

Lou Montecalvo (gone to be with Jesus)
Founding and Overseeing Pastor of Redeemer Ministries
www.redeemertemple.com

We met Joe and Stephanie DeMott several years ago in conjunction with ministry efforts of one of the ministries with which we cooperate. Although each restored couple's restoration story is unique we found that our journeys to restoration and healing were similar in many ways. We have spent a lot of time on several occasions "comparing notes" and praising God for what He has done in all of our lives and especially for our marriage restorations.

Joe and Stephanie have a compelling testimony of what God can accomplish in a devastated marriage if either the husband or wife will choose to believe in and hold fast to their covenant marriage vows. Their commitment to marriage healing and restoration for not only themselves but all marriages that they can touch is a calling from God. They are truly missionaries to marriages around the world.

Don't read their story just as one of how badly two people can treat each other in the midst of marital strife. Instead read it for the glory they give God for His protection, guidance and safe keeping on their journey back from the brink.

Rex and Carolyn Johnson
Covenant Keepers Inc.

www.covenantkeepersinc.org

"I've heard many testimonies of marital redemptions over the years. Joe and Stephanie's is one of most dramatic. Moving from abuse and adultery to love and strong covenant is truly a miracle of God. I pray that reading this booklet will be a turning point for many couples facing similar situations. God does indeed raise the dead!"

R. Loren Sandford, (Gone to be with Jesus)
Senior pastor New Song Church and Ministries (Denver, Colorado), author, prophetic voice and conference speaker
www.newsongchurchandministries.org

Coming soon "The Blood Cry's Out" Joe and Stephanie's testimony of Joe's career on the Denver Police Department and God's work while he worked in the Homicide Unit

There are many videos also available on Missionaries2Marriages YouTube and Rumble channels

Now Go and Do!

Thank you for taking time to read this guide and more importantly seek God's heart for your ministry. Missionaries2Marriages is excited to partner with you as you do what God is calling you to do. Whether you are working directly with Missionaries2Marriages or using our resources in your own ministry, we pray that God would use you in amazing ways to help bring restoration and hope to marriages and families all over the world. We encourage you to reach out to us with our contact information below.

Directors: Joe and Stephanie DeMott
- Office Phone: 303-465-0342
- Cell Phone: 720-351-6211
- Email: demott@missionaries2marriages.com
- Mailing Address: PO BOX 7832
  Broomfield, Co 80021

Executive Assistant/Director of Media and Communication: Leslie DeMott
- Cell Phone: 951-204-1091
- Email: leslie@missionaries2marriages.com

Notes